I, The Universe

Kat Bliss

BookLeaf Publishing

India | USA | UK

Presentation by *BookLeaf Publishing*

Web: www.bookleafpub.com

E-mail: info@bookleafpub.com

ISBN: 9789358317473

First edition 2024

DEDICATION

To my wonderful spouse, for teaching me how
to find joy in myself again.

Oblivion Speaks

Empty bottles litter the room.
Cigarette smoke hangs in the air.
"I love you" sits on the table,
"I'm sorry" lays on the floor.
Blue lights flash through the windows.
Dinner burns in the kitchen.
The front door swings open.
Oblivion pours in.

The Forest

Fairies laughed in the clearing
As I wandered through the trees.
Lightning bugs fluttered around me.
The breeze flowed through my hair.
The sun sparkled down through the leaves.
Then the clouds came.
Darkness fell over the forest.
The fairies screamed in delight at my terror.
Their voices pierced the peace.
The lightning bugs tangled in my hair.
They pulled me towards the clearing.
The forest floor opened up.
And swallowed me whole.

A Wasteland

I am a wasteland
Of broken memories
And bad choices.
Shattered memories
Like shards of glass.
Broken and Forgotten.

The Storm

The wind drowns out my thoughts
As it screams around me.
The rain hides my tears
As it runs down my face and neck.
The thunder covers the noise of my screams
And the lightning shows my broken mind to the
world.

Truth and Eyes

I've forgotten their eyes.
The kind ones
And the hard ones
And the ones that held lies.
I've forgotten the truth.
I've learned the lies
They forced upon me
As they drowned out my voice.

The Act of Being

I have performed my life
Instead of experiencing it.
My consciousness floated away,
Into my own little Universe.
I acted how I was supposed to
And I forgot it all.

The Haunting

The shadow peers around the corner
When she thinks I can't see her.
She's looking for a way to remind me she's there.
I can't lose her.
She follows me everywhere.
I can't confront her.
She disappears.
She's the ghost of my mistakes
And she won't ever leave me.

The Death of the Stars

I've done it again.
I've let the cracks show,
And the darkness slips out.
Shame and judgement and self-hate start to seep
in.
The stars in the darkness dim to nothing.

The Darkest Night

The world is full of so much darkness.
The weight of it all
Is crushing me.

Black Holes

There is a black hole.
It takes everything inside me.
All of my hope,
My memories,
They disappear into the void.

Innocence in Damnation

A white lie
And good intentions
Will bring the world
Crashing down to the ground

Tape Me Up

I feel like I'm faking.
I feel like I'm fading.
I hide my sins beneath my scars
And hope my bandages are enough
To hold me together.

Breaking Down

The floods are rising.
It has rained for days.
The sky is dark and heavy with the clouds.
The rolling thunder is all that breaks
The silence of rainfall.

Curse of My Life

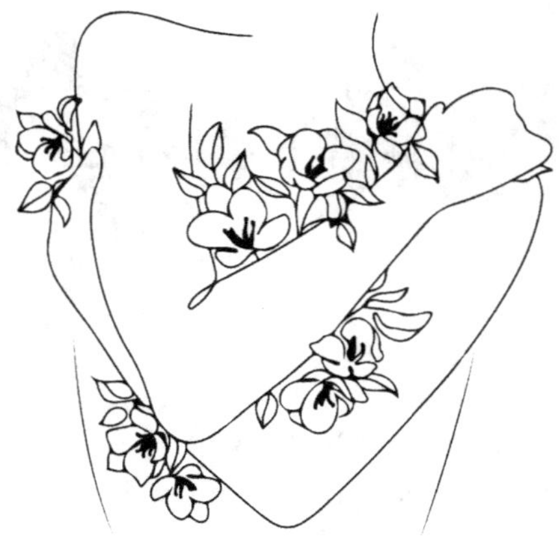

She is trying to make herself heard
In a world that smothers her voice.
She is trying to be seen
In a world that makes her invisible.
Sentience was bad enough
But I've been cursed with self-awareness.

Strongholds and Fortresses

To know me
Is to hate me
And what I've become.
I am a fortress.
Stronger than my years
Colder than my time.
There is no space for apathy
In the stronghold of my heart.

The Hidden Mist

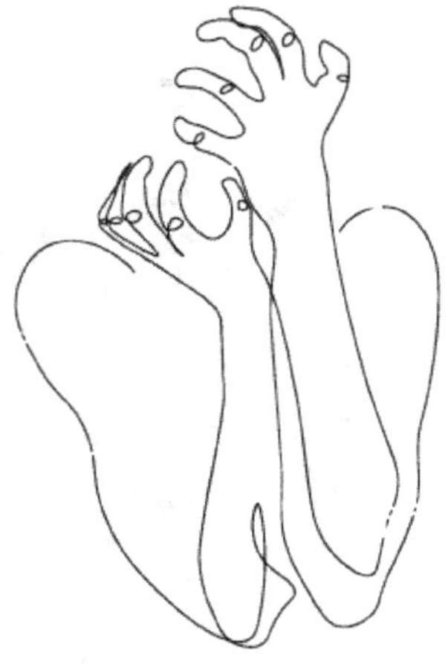

I live in the shadows
Hiding in alleys and lonely corners.
A black mist in the wind
Giving voice to the darkness.

A Heartless Void

My heart is the void
Where good intentions go
To die.

Lose Yourself in Me

My smile is a jinx
My heart is a curse
I have never-ending patience
But my rage snaps me in half.
To be loved by me
Is to lose yourself to my darkness.
It will drown you
And I can do nothing to stop it.

Rush of the Fall

Sometimes I climb too high
Just to feel alive as I fall.
I see the fear on your face.
I see you trying to catch me.
I just want to feel alive.

Volcanoes Explode

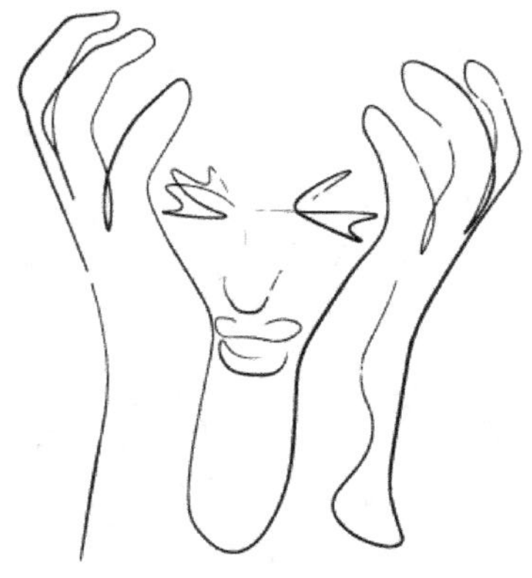

The lava bubbles
Just below the surface.
Looking for any small fissure
To seep out from.
Yet, it explodes.

It explodes from me.
Leaving my body
In ruins.

Spring Meadows

Small
Drops
Falling on a frozen lake.

They
Don't
Melt any of it away.

To Protect You

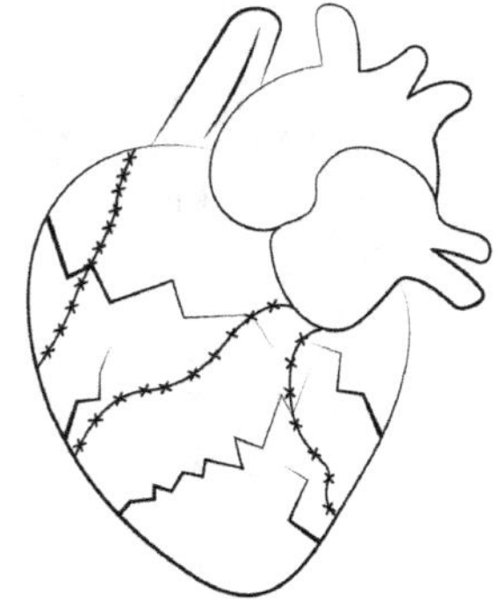

I pick myself apart at the seams.
Pull out all my stitches.
Rearrange my wounds
So you can't see them.

The Emergency

I left with the sirens and the lights
My love and trust in the rearview mirror.

The truth was shielded by my innocence.
Your evil hidden by my faith.

The Cemetery

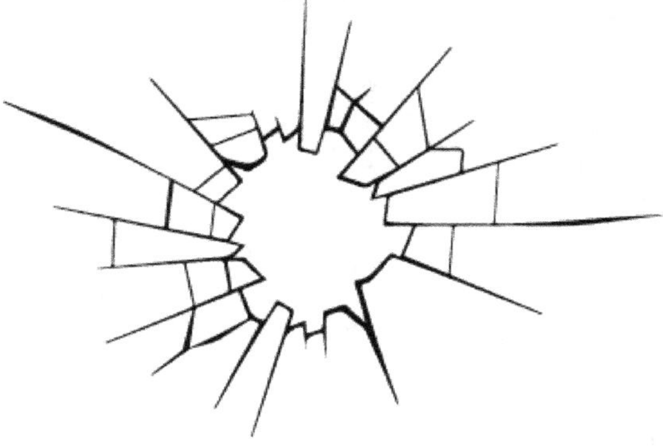

My body is not a temple.

It is a crypt
Filled with cobwebs
And black memories.

Light streams in
Through the cracks in the stone.
One by one, I cover up the cracks.
And I return to the shadows.

The Sacrifice

The moon passes over the sun
It blocks out all light
Shadows are thrown over the world
Do we need a sacrifice?
To whom and for what?
Redemption?

I cannot control the panic
That washes over the crowd.
They hoist their sacrifice
Up to their shoulders
And they toss her into the lake.

She struggles.
Her screams are drowned out by
The waves crashing on the shore.
The crowd watches with hope
As she disappears beneath the surface.

The moon releases the light.
Sunshine glimmers on the lake
The panic fades.
The crowd disperses.
And I am left to pull the body from the lake.

Queen of Darkness

She moves in a cloud of shadows
The darkness draped over her shoulders.
The sunflowers wilted and drooped
As she floated by.
The secret stars shone through her skin
But the darkness was too heavy
For the stars to release her.

The Firefighter in Me

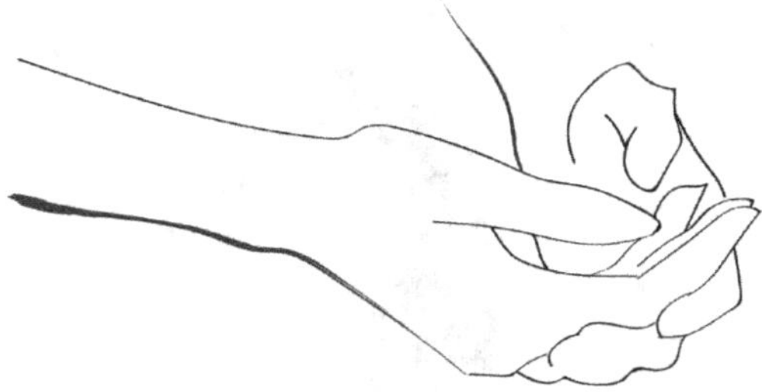

I'm doing it again.
I'm putting out fires for everyone else.
Letting my own burn up inside me.
I can feel the flames
Licking at my heart and soul
Turning them to ash.

Let Me Feel

Sometimes I don't want to be better.
I want to feel sad, angry, numb.
I want to feel it and name it and know it
Before I stuff it back in its box.

Shadows

They paint me in black
Marring my heart and my soul.
They cover up my voice and my dreams.
I am left with the outline of a person.
A shadow of what I once was.
A space where I once existed.

Thunder in Me

My head is full of clouds.
Every thought a deafening thunderclap
The lightning flashes in my eyes.
And rain falls from my heart.

The Birth of Light

Silent nights and tear-stained pillows
Passing cars splash light on the wall.
The remnants of you
Lay scattered on the floor.
Dismantled by the truth of you.
They were only a mirage
An illusion of you.
Distortions of childish hope.
But no longer
Do I believe in you.

Rising Again

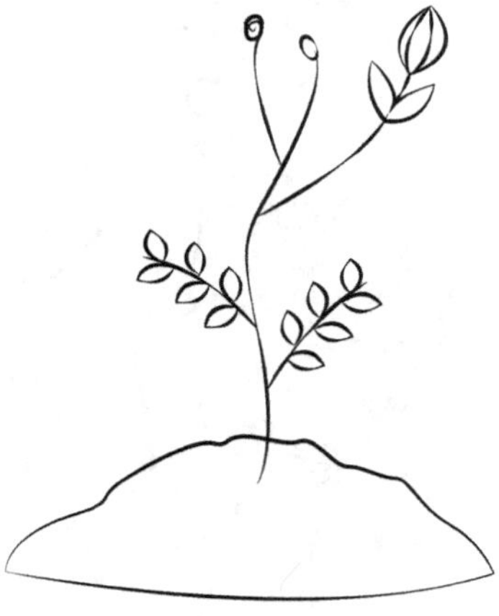

Do not outstay
Your welcome here.
I will burn you
With one touch.
I will watch the
Burning embers of you
Blow away on a
Phantom breeze.

Do not outstay
Your welcome here.
You do not own
Any part of me.
You are here
On my kindness
And I will ruin you.

Finding Peace in Pain

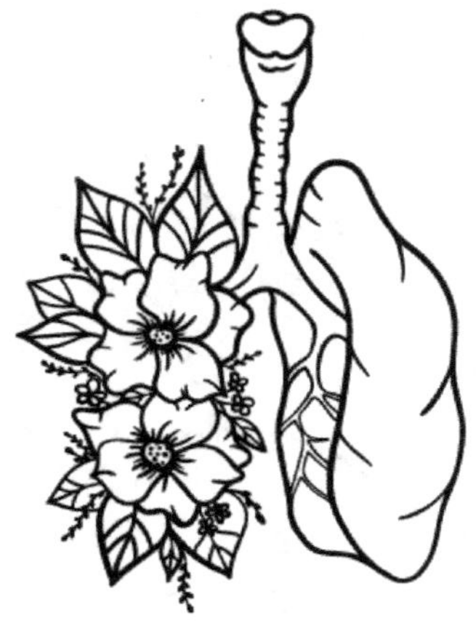

I've learned to love the darkness.
It's quiet and it's warm.
It is no longer filled with
The horrors of my imagination.
I am no longer haunted by
The things that lurk behind light switches.

Learning to Breathe

There is fire in my veins
And ice in my heart.
I've built a wall around my body
With the stones they've thrown at me.
You made a crack in the wall
With your smile and your eyes.
You reached through the gap
With gentleness and kindness.
The fire in me soothed.
My ice melted.
I started to come alive again.

I am a Phoenix

I was born to be majestic.
A phoenix rising from the ashes
Every time a dagger is thrust
Into my heart.
So you don't get to hold a gun to my head
And tell me I'm a simple girl.
I was born from ashes
And I will be again.

Remembering Peace

Waves crash against the wall.
Sea salt sprays my face.
It calms the fire in me.
It settles my soul.
Something moves in the water,
A soft movement in the waves.
The snout of a seal pops up
And dips back down into the water.
All of that freedom in one small action
Reminds me I'm part of something bigger.
It stops me from sinking into my own little
bubble
And I remember to breathe again.

Relapse

Whoever said all is fair
In love and war
Was clearly delusional.
Many wars have been fought and won
On the pillars of
Deceit and distrust.
The War in me is no exception.
The Platoons of Mind
March on the encampment of Heart
Leaving destruction in their wake
No Heart is left
But a limp and bloody pulp
That cannot beat for itself.

So no,
War is not fair
And neither is love.
It leaves you broken,
Bruised and bloody.

The Last Call

The line is dead.
Nothing but a soft buzzing.
Your voice fades to nothing.

All memories of you are gone.
That final phone call disappears.
All that's left is the buzzing.

Explore the Unknown

What is out there
In the darkness?
Is it worse
Than the emptiness inside?
What is hiding
In the shadows?
Can I survive it?

Mr. Deniability

He stood at the door
With his hat in his hands.
His eyes sought my forgiveness.

His lips held his lies.
His indiscretions burned a hole in my heart
And I slammed the door in his face.

He slammed his fists against the door.
His hat fell to the ground
His eyes burned with fury
His lips screamed his lies.
I covered my ears and closed my eyes
And I buried him deep inside my soul.

Standing on the Edge

Can I move as close as possible
To the edge of the silence of Death
Without committing myself wholly
And being thrown into the abyss
From which no one returns?

I Need a Fairytale

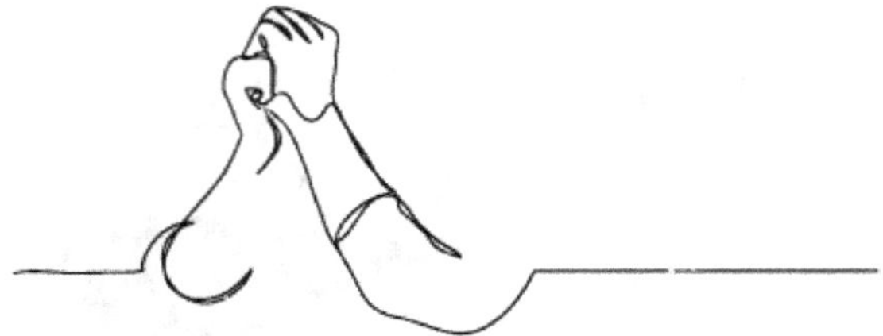

Please tell me a story.
A fairytale of sorts.
One where the princess befriends her dragon
And rescues herself from her tower.

One where the princess reclaims her throne
And forgives those who took it from her.

Free Me From Myself

I have been twisted and distorted.
Made into something I don't want to be.
The darkness in the void.

You are light and hope.
Beams shining through the cracks in
The walls around me.

You pull at the bricks
As I scratch from inside
And I breathe in the taste of
Freedom.

The History of Me

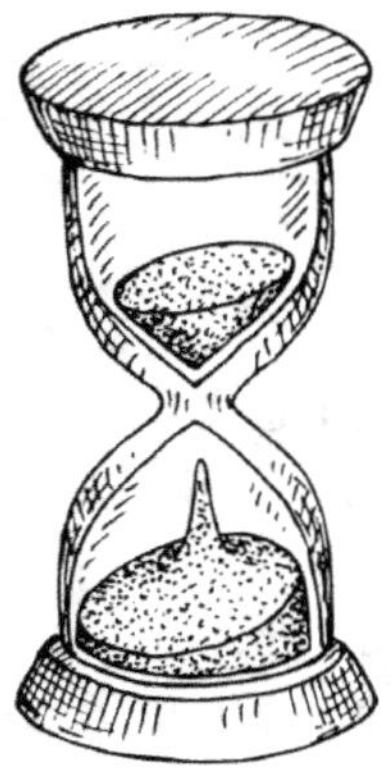

There is nothing unique in me.
I am the product of all those who have come
before me.

I know nothing new.
I am the words of the poets.
The essence of tragedies
I am the great wars
And the great loves
That I have never known.

In me are the clouds that have rained
The volcanoes that have erupted
And the rivers that flow to the sea.

I am stardust and armadas
I am time itself
And I will repeat through the ages.

Finding the Truth

The journey from anger
To defeat and acceptance
Is a road I know too well.
My resentment grows
As the story unfolds.

And I learn the
Truth of myself.

Resolve

Stay soft.
Don't let the world turn you cold like stone.
And shatter you into a million pieces.

Destiny

Am I destined to live with
One foot in the grave
And my head in the clouds?
My heart on my sleeve
And my future in your eyes?

Driving Away

Taillights disappear over the hill
And I am filled with relief.
The pain recedes with you.
I can close the door on you.

My Little Girl

I turned to face
The demons in my past
And all I saw
Was a small girl
Full of love.

Drowned in pain
Weighed down by grief
And desperate to be seen.

Flashlights in the Dark

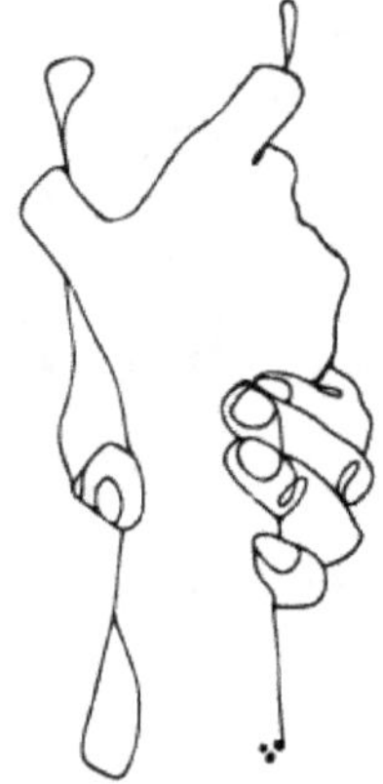

You share in my darkness
With one of your own
We fight the same battles
Side by side, and often alone
My darkness comes in shades of grey.

And I'm sorry that they cloud
Your view of the world.
I don't mean any harm
I'm trying to help you
More than I can help myself.

Partners in Pain

Our wounds run deep
We have matching scars.
Words alone could never
Heal what we've felt.
But with your hand in mine
The wounds close over
And the scars begin to fade.

My Mosaic

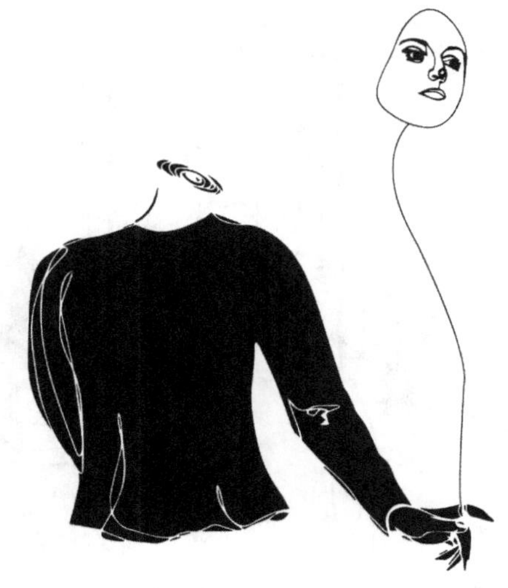

My soul resides in the
Very depths of me.
A place light barely reaches.
It lives with my nightmares
And my fears.

The hopes turned into failures
And my most righteous anger.
My soul is a mosaic
Of the things no one will know.

A Message to the Past

Your sacrifice
Has become my oath.
The pain you felt
Will not be for nothing.
Rest easy, little one.

I will carry on for us both.

A Message for the Future

Life is not a straight line.
The sun can be bright and the wind calm
For months, maybe years.
And suddenly a hurricane blows in.
No one can predict exactly when a hurricane
will hit.
Even the weatherman can be wrong.
But it doesn't mean the sun won't ever be back.
Keep believing you can heal.
Because life is not a straight line.

Ocean Depths

I am afraid of the ocean.
How it rips me from my feet.
It hides depths in the darkness.
It is a reflection of my soul.

But I would jump off a pier for you.
I would swim the darkest depths for you.
I'd risk drowning to pull you back to the surface.
For you, I'd be braver than my fears.

Glimmers of Hope

In the darkest corner
Of the deepest abyss
There is a tiny glimmer
Clinging to life against all odds.
That glimmer has a name

Its name is Hope.

My Home

The lights of the city are calling me home…
But home isn't there anymore.
Home is your hair
Your lips
Your hands
Your smell.
Home is where the heart is.
My heart is with you.

Worthy of the Sun

My love
The sun doesn't shine just because
I said it does.
The earth doesn't turn just because
I noticed it.

You don't have worth just because
I said so.
All I did was acknowledge it.
This is what I mean
When I say
You are worth it.

Stargazing

We lay on the grass
Looking up at the night
Your fingers in my hair
A smile on my lips
You wondered why I wasn't talking.

I was busy naming stars after you.

My Galaxy

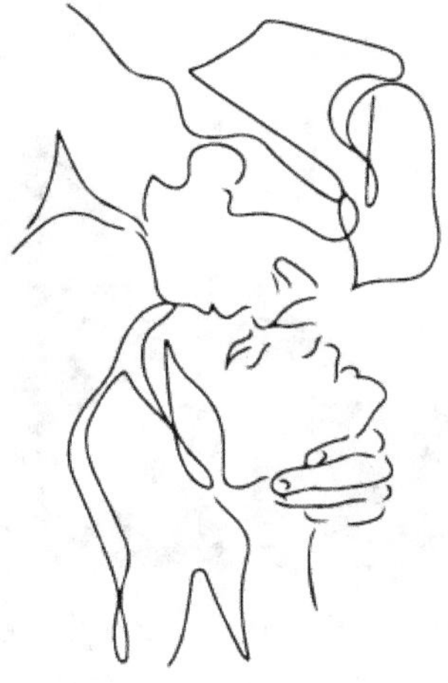

You light up my heart
With the sparkle in your eyes.
Your arms hold me tight
And glue my cracks back together
With your golden warmth.

You've built me a space
Where I have peace to heal.
The stars in me start to shine again.
An inferno of hope
That you can hold in your hands.

I, the Universe

A silent breeze swirled through the leaves
As I looked up at the clear, dark sky.
I watched the stars come to life in the night.
The door was open to galaxies and universes
And I wondered at my own significance.

Billions of people and even more creatures
On this one little planet alone.
What am I, but a speck
Of nothing in everything.

Then I felt your hand creep into mine.
And the stars condensed into your eyes.
A galaxy was in your heart.
A universe in your soul.
I may be nothing to the Universe.

A small part in the motions of Everything
Lost in the movements of All.
But with you, I am whole.
With you, I am everything.
I find myself in you.
I am a Universe.